Wedding Music
for Solo Cello

by Katherine Curatolo

© 2013 BY MEL BAY PUBLICATIONS, INC. ALL RIGHTS RESERVED.
WWW.MELBAY.COM

Introduction

Written for solo cello without need for piano accompaniment, this collection contains straightforward arrangements of the selections most frequently requested for wedding ceremonies. Inside you will find traditional wedding favorites as well as beautiful classical pieces to create an elegant musical experience. The pieces are loosely grouped according to their traditional or suggested usage: prelude music, processionals, music for the ceremony, and recessionals. These labels are fluid, and songs can be used in various ways as a part of the wedding ceremony.

Table of Contents

Air
from *Water Music*

George Frideric Handel
Arranged K. Curatolo

The Ash Grove

Traditional
Arranged K. Curatolo

Arioso

Johann Sebastian Bach
Arranged K. Curatolo

Adagio

(Last time rit.)

Ode to Joy

Ludwig van Beethoven
Arranged K. Curatolo

Sheep May Safely Graze

from *Cantata No. 208*

Johann Sebastian Bach
Arranged K. Curatolo

Largo
from *The Four Seasons–Winter*

Antonio Vivaldi
Arranged K. Curatolo

Allegro
from *The Four Seasons–Spring*

Antonio Vivaldi
Arranged K. Curatolo

Jesu, Joy of Man's Desiring

Johann Sebastian Bach
Arranged K. Curatolo

12

Canon in D

Johann Pachelbel
Arranged K. Curatolo

Andante

Intermezzo
from *Cavelleria Rusticana*

Pietro Mascagni
Arranged K. Curatolo

Trumpet Voluntary

Jeremiah Clarke
Arranged K. Curatolo

Bridal Chorus
from *Lohengrin*

Richard Wagner
Arranged K. Curatolo

Ave Maria

Franz Schubert
Arranged K. Curatolo

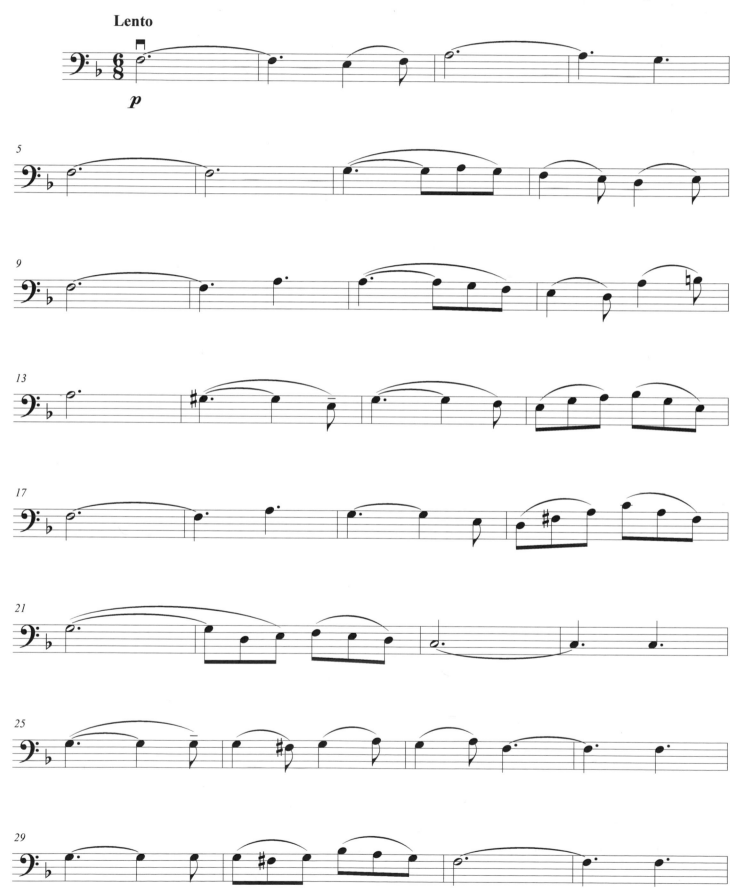

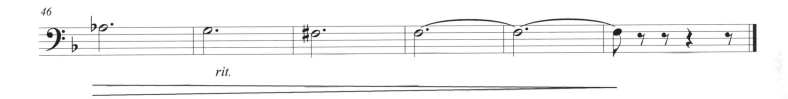

Bist du bei mir

Gottfried Heinrich Stölzel
Arranged K. Curatolo

Air on the G String

Johann Sebastian Bach
Arranged K. Curatolo

Ave Verum Corpus

Wolfgang Amadeus Mozart
Arranged K. Curatolo

Largo
from *Xerxes*

George Frideric Handel
Arranged K. Curatolo

Wachet auf
(Sleepers Awake)

Johann Sebastian Bach
Arranged K. Curatolo

rit.

Wedding March

from *A Midsummer Night's Dream*

Felix Mendelssohn
Arranged K. Curatolo

Allegro

Trumpet Tune

Henry Purcell
Arranged K. Curatolo

Rondeau

Jean–Joseph Mouret
Arranged K. Curatolo

rit.

Hornpipe
from *Water Music*

George Frideric Handel
Arranged K. Curatolo

La Rejouissance

George Frideric Handel
Arranged K. Curatolo

Last time rit.

D.C.

WWW.MELBAY.COM